FAMOUS AMERICANS:
George Washington
and
Abraham Lincoln

by
Maria Fleming

SCHOLASTIC
PROFESSIONAL BOOKS

NEW YORK • TORONTO • LONDON • AUCKLAND • SYDNEY

Acknowledgments:
Page 37: "To Meet Mr. Lincoln" by Eve Merriam. From JAMBOREE Rhymes For All Times by Eve Merriam. Copyright © 1962, 1964, 1966, 1973, 1984 by Eve Merriam. © by Eve Merriam. Reprinted by permission of Marian Reiner. Poster: "President's Day" by Myra Cohn Livingston from CELEBRATIONS by Myra Cohn Livingston (Holiday House). Copyright © 1985 by Myra Cohn Livingston. Reprinted by permission of Marian Reiner for the artist.

A special thanks to Jim Halverson and Carol Pugliano for their play, *Dreaming of George and Abe*.

Cover design by Vincent Ceci and Jaime Lucero

Cover photographs courtesy of the Library of Congress

Cover illustration by Stephanie Petersen

Interior design by Ellen Matlach Hassell
for Boultinghouse & Boultinghouse, Inc.

Interior illustrations by Maxie Chambliss and Manuel Rivera

ISBN 0-590-53550-1

Copyright © 1996 by Maria Fleming

All rights reserved.

Printed in the U.S.A.

12 11 10 9 8 7 6 5 4 3 2 1 1 2 3 4 5 6/9

TABLE OF CONTENTS

Perhaps the strongest feature in his character was prudence, never acting until every circumstance, every consideration, was maturely weighed; refraining if he saw a doubt, but, when once decided, going through with his purpose, whatever obstacles opposed.

"His integrity was most pure, his justice the most inflexible I have ever known . . .

"He was, indeed, in every sense of the words, a wise, a good and a great man . . . On the whole, his character was, in its mass, perfect . . . it may truly be said, that never did nature and fortune combine more perfectly to make a man great . . . "

—Thomas Jefferson, paying
tribute to George Washington

There is no new thing to be said about Lincoln. There is no new thing to be said of the mountains, or of the sea, or of the stars. The years go their way, but the same old mountains lift their granite shoulders above the drifting clouds; the same mysterious sea beats upon the shore; the same silent stars keep holy vigil above a tired world. But to the mountains and the sea and stars men turn forever in unwearied homage. And thus with Lincoln. For he was a mountain in grandeur of soul, he was a sea in deep undervoice of mystic loneliness, he was a star in steadfast purity of purpose and service. And he abides."

—Homer Koch, a congressman
from Kansas, paying tribute to
Abraham Lincoln

CHAPTER 1

Getting to Know George

A Legendary Life

Everybody knows the story of young George Washington, his handy hatchet, and the ill-fated cherry tree. Many people also know the story is more fable than fact. George did have a hatchet that he was fond of using, but the story was invented by his early biographer, Mason Locke Weems, to prove Washington's noble character—his inability to tell a lie—from an early age.

Though the story is a fabrication, reports of Washington's upstanding character ring true. His integrity, honesty, sound judgment, and deep sense of duty to his country are part of why he is remembered today as one of our nation's greatest presidents.

Growing Up in Virginia

Much of George Washington's childhood has been mythologized, but in fact, little is known of his early boyhood. What is known is that he was born on February 22, 1732, in Westmoreland County, Virginia, to Augustine Washington and his second wife, Mary Ball Washington. His father was a tobacco farmer, and George spent his boyhood on a 260-acre plantation called Ferry Farm. The farm overlooked the Rappahannock River, where George fished and swam and sailed as a youth. Robust and athletic, George Washington loved to ride horses, and became a skilled equestrian. At Ferry Farm, he also learned how to manage a plantation. Although he would later become a celebrated military leader and president, Washington always considered himself a farmer first.

Family Life

George Washington came from a large family that included three younger brothers, a younger sister, and two older half brothers from his father's previous marriage. When Washington was 11, his father died. George's older half-brother Lawrence then became very important in young George's life, filling the roles of father figure, role model, and close friend. George made frequent trips to Mount Vernon, Lawrence's home on the Potomac River which he would one day inherit.

A Rural Education

Little is known about George Washington's schooling, but most likely, he received a basic education in reading, writing, and arithmetic at a small farm school from the age of 8 till the age of 14 or 15. Some notebooks of Washington's do survive, in which he wrote his lessons. In one notebook, he copied a list of 110 "Rules of Civility and Decent Behaviour in Company and Conversation" which noted such lessons in etiquette as:

It's unbecoming to stoop much to one's meat. Keep your fingers clean and when foul wipe them on a corner of your table napkin.

While the rules sound funny today, it is believed young George took them quite seriously; all his life, he was concerned about his character, and took pains to preserve his reputation.

Forging a Career

As a young man, George—who had an aptitude for math—began studying how to survey land. By the age of 16, he was doing a brisk business as a land surveyor, acquiring his own land with his earnings. By the time he was 20, Washington owned more than 2,300 acres of land.

A Change in Direction

Around the same time, his beloved brother Lawrence fell sick and died. Lawrence had once served in the military, and Washington remembered with interest his brother's war stories. Following in his older brother's footsteps, he joined the Virginia militia, which was a group of volunteer soldiers that helped the British army defend America's western frontier. It was a step

that paved the way for a long and celebrated military career, and—ultimately—George Washington's election as the first President of the United States.

STUDENT ACTIVITIES

 What Do You Know About George?

Children will most likely have some prior knowledge about George Washington. To tap into this knowledge, and to create a place for asking and answering questions about George Washington, make a "KWL" chart. Divide a bulletin board into three columns, making the third one twice as large as the first two. Label the first column, "What We Know About Washington"; label the second, "What We Want to Learn About Washington"; and the third, "What We've Learned About Washington." On page 8, you'll find tri-cornered hat patterns. Children can use these to record prior knowledge, questions, and discoveries for the chart. After you've completed your study of Washington, look back at

the first column. Did children have any misinformation about our nation's first president? Discuss reasons for this.

★The Life of a Leader

For a ready reference on Washington, children can make a time line highlighting the key events in his life. When assembled, the patterns on pages 9–10 will make a time line that resembles the nation's first flag. (Legend has it that Washington helped Betsy Ross design the flag that includes a stripe and a star for each of the 13 colonies/states.) Children can make the time lines on their own, in a group, or as a class. Make a photocopy of pages 9 and 10. (If you are making a class time line, you may want to enlarge the images for a more prominent display.)

Begin by having children cut apart the sentence strips on reproducible page 10. Each strip describes a key event in Washington's life and represents one stripe on the flag. Children can put the facts in chronological order on the flag pattern on page 9, beginning with Washington's birth at the bottom and ending with his death at the top. After children have double-checked the order of events, they can glue the stripes in place.

To make the activity more challenging for older children, cover the dates before photocopying the page. Challenge children to find the date for each event before putting it in its correct place on the flag. You may want to use the time line as the center of a bulletin board on George Washington's life. Children can add information, quotations, stories, and other materials as they learn more about Washington.

★ A Boy Named George

On pages 11–12 you'll find a pattern for making a mini-biography that focuses on George Washington's boyhood. Make a double-sided photocopy of these pages, being careful not to invert the copy on the reverse side. Then children can:

☆ Place the paper on the desk so that panels A and B face up.

☆ Cut panels A and B apart along the solid line.

☆ Lay panel B on top of panel A so that the pages of the book are in the right order.

☆ Fold the stacked panels along the dashed line and staple along the left edge to secure the pages.

After children read the book, create a class chart comparing Washington's childhood with that of children living today.

★ A Big Brother

The mini-book mentions George Washington's special relationship with his older brother and role model, Lawrence. After reading the mini-book together, photocopy and distribute reproducible page 13, which asks children to think about someone they respect and admire. Allow time for children to share their writings and drawings with the class.

★ The Rules of Good Behavior

All his life, Washington was concerned with his reputation and wanted to make a good impression on people. And indeed, he did—a good impression that has endured the test of time. On page 14 are some of the rules for good behavior that he copied into his notebook as a boy. Provide each child with a copy of the page. Talk about the way the rules are worded, what they mean, and why some of the language sounds funny. Help children reword the rules as they might be said today. Ask children to add to the page their own ideas for behaving well. Allow time for children to share their ideas, and compare Washington's concern for his reputation to their own. Do they care what others think of them? Why or why not? How would they like to be regarded by other people?

As a follow-up activity, students may want to use George Washington's rules as a model for creating "Rules of Civility and Decent Behaviour in Company and Conversation" to follow in your classroom. The rules might be phrased as Washington would have written them. For example, "When standing on line, do not jostle or push," or "Sit quietly for all guests and visitors, even when you don't feel like it."

What Do You Know About George?

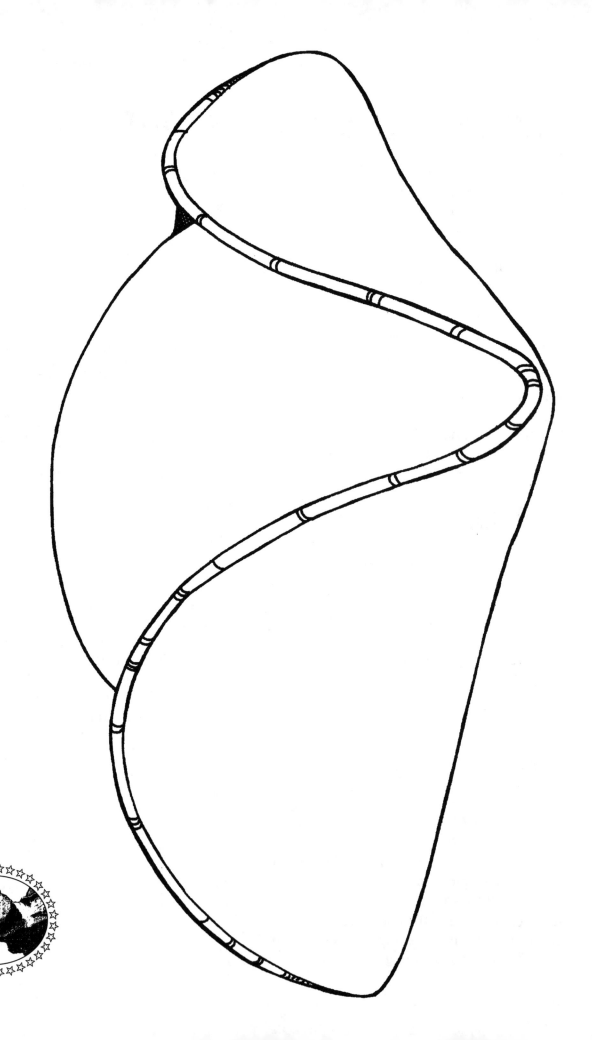

Name

George
Washington's
Life

The Life of a Leader

1792 Washington is reelected for a second term as President.

1783 The American Revolution ends. Washington returns home to live at Mount Vernon.

1787 Washington is elected president of the Constitutional Convention. This group writes the U.S. Constitution.

1799 George Washington dies on December 14. He is 67 years old.

1789 George Washington is elected the first President of the United States of America.

1797 Washington retires from the job of President. He goes back home to his farm, Mount Vernon.

1781 The battle of Yorktown is fought. It is a big victory for America.

1743 Washington's father dies.

1749 Washington becomes a surveyor in Virginia. He makes his living measuring land.

1732 George Washington is born in Virginia on February 22.

1759 He marries a widow named Martha Custis.

1775 Washington becomes the commander in chief of the Continental Army during the American Revolution.

1752 Washington's brother, Lawrence, dies. George joins the Virginia militia.

He would grow up to lead his country to freedom. He would grow up to be the first President of the United States.

A Boy Named George

The year was 1732. The place was Virginia. On February 22 of that year, the Washington family had a baby boy. They named him George—George Washington.

George loved to visit his half-brother Lawrence. Lawrence lived nearby in a big house on a river. He taught George how shoot and hunt. Together they would swim and fish and sail in the river.

But George Washington didn't think about any of this. He was too busy helping out on the farm where he lived. The farm had cows and pigs and chickens. It had fields of tobacco. And it had horses—George loved to ride the horses.

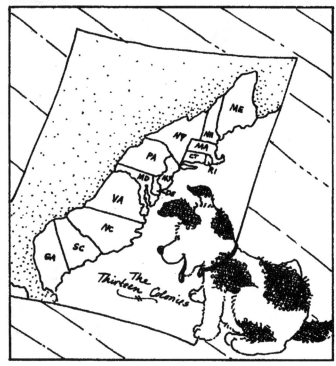

In those days the United States wasn't yet a nation. It was made up of colonies. These colonies were ruled by Great Britain.

2

All in all, George Washington was much like other boys. But he would grow up to be a man who stood apart from all other men.

7

Like other boys on other farms, George Washington went to a small school near his home. There he learned to read and write. He liked math, but had trouble with spelling.

4

George had a big family. He had three younger brothers, and a younger sister. His father had been married before, so George had two older half-brothers, too.

5

A Big Brother

George Washington spent hours with his brother Lawrence. They rode horses and talked together. When George grew up, he became a soldier, just like Lawrence.

Is there a friend or family member you look up to? What do you like to do with this person?

Draw a picture to show what you do.

1. Why do you look up to this person? _____

_____

_____

2. In what ways would you like to be like him or her? _____

_____

_____

The Rules of Good Behavior

Do you think it's important to have good manners? George Washington did. When he was young, he wrote down rules for acting politely in his notebook. He tried hard to follow them.

> ## Rules of Civility and Decent Behaviour in Company and Conversation
>
> 1. Sleep not when others speak. Sit not when others stand. Speak not when you should hold your peace. Walk not when others stop.
>
> 2. Turn not your back to others especially in speaking.
>
> 3. While you are talking, point not with your finger.
>
> 4. Do not laugh too much or too loud in public.
>
> 5. Being set at a meal, scratch not; neither spit, cough, nor blow your nose, except if there is necessity for it.

Write down three good manners that you follow.

1. _____

2. _____

3. _____

CHAPTER 2

The Father of His Country

Military Man

In his twenties, Washington gained military experience during the French and Indian War—a conflict between Great Britain and France over land rights in the American wilderness. At 26, Washington retired from military service and married a young widow named Martha Dandridge Custis. Martha had two children, Jackie and Patsy, from an earlier marriage. Together, the family settled at Mount Vernon, Lawrence's plantation on the Potomac River. For the next 16 years, Washington busied himself with expanding his land holdings, managing his crops and estate, and entertaining guests at his magnificent home. He also served in the Virginia legislature, gaining his first political experience.

Duty Calls

While Washington was leading the life of a country gentleman, hostilities were building between the colonies and Great Britain. When war finally broke out in 1775, Washington was elected commander in chief of the Continental Army.

It was a tough assignment: the colonial army was undisciplined and untrained. The troops lacked food, clothing, and ammunition. Compared to the well-outfitted British forces, it was a ragtag band of men. Desertion was commonplace. Sometimes it was all Washington could do to hold the troops together, and he was often discouraged. He wrote, "Such is my situation that if I were to wish the bitterest curse to an enemy on this side of the grave, I should put him in my stead with my feelings."

Victory at Last

Still, the American forces persevered, and the British finally surrendered to Washington at Yorktown, Virginia, in 1781. It was the last major battle of the Revolution, and a peace treaty was signed a year and a half later.

Duty Calls Again

George Washington left the war a hero. Some of the soldiers who had served under him even suggested that he be named king. But the idea horrified Washington, who had just spent almost a decade fighting to free the colonies from the King of England's rule. Once again, he retired to a quiet life at Mount Vernon, only to be called back into the service of his country a few years later. In 1787, Washington attended and was elected president of the Constitutional Convention, where he presided over the long and arduous business of drawing up a plan of government for the newly formed nation. In 1789, after the Constitution was ratified, the 57-year-old retired general was elected as first President of the United States.

Mr. President

Washington accepted the position with considerable doubt about his own abilities. However, despite his reluctance, he provided strong leadership and was known for his sound judgment and decisive action on issues. As the first President, George Washington set the tone for the nation's highest office: he declined to be called "His Highness," preferring instead "Mr. President," to make it clear he was a representative of the people and not a monarch.

Home at Last

Washington served two terms as President, refusing the suggestion of a third to retire once more to his beloved Mount Vernon. He was 65 years old when he left office and gladly exchanged the troubling duties of President for the peaceful life of a farmer. He attended to the upkeep of his home and oversaw his fields, riding out on horseback each morning to inspect some part of his 7,600-acre plantation. It was after one of these rides, on a rainy December morning in 1799, that Washington fell ill. What started as a sore throat quickly worsened. Two days later, on December 14, 1799, George Washington died at the age of 67.

LITERATURE LAUNCHERS
To create a historical context for learning about George Washington's role in the American Revolution, you may want to share with students *Sam the Minuteman* and *George the Drummer Boy*, both by Nathaniel Benchley (HarperCollins, 1987), which describe the war from the American and British perspectives, respectively. *Buttons for General Washington* by Peter and Connie Roop (Carolrhoda, 1986) is another good choice for shared reading.

★ General George

Share with students some of the background information about Washington's military career, and invite them to find out more about the causes and conflicts of the American Revolution. On page 19 is a song, entitled "General George," that recounts some of the Revolution's key events: Washington's famous trip across the Delaware River and surprise attack of the Hessian soldiers at Trenton on Christmas Day (December 25, 1776); the suffering at Valley Forge, Pennsylvania, where Washington saw his hungry, ill-housed, and ill-clad troops through a bitter winter (1777–1778); the French-assisted defeat of Cornwallis and his 8,000 troops at Yorktown, Virginia, in the last major battle of the Revolution (1781).

Sing the song to the tune of "Yankee Doodle." "Yankee Doodle" was first sung by the well-dressed and well-trained British military to make fun of the ragtag colonial army during the French and Indian War. "Yankee" referred to the colonists, and "Doodle" meant "do-little" or "silly." However, the joke backfired as Americans embraced the lively tune and played it in their own camps. During the Revolution, it became America's first patriotic song.

After children sing the song, divide the class into groups and have students find out more about the events mentioned, as well as other facts about the Revolution. Children can write additional verses as they find out more about the war and General Washington's role in it.

★ Marching Toward Victory

George Washington would have been familiar with the practice of "mustering up"—a term that refers to the lining up of colonial soldiers into civil or military formations. Troops responded to signals—such as a drumbeat or a whistle—in these drills. Colonial troops would sometimes drill and march to the song "Yankee Doodle" because of its strong beat and patriotic quality. Students may enjoy trying to "muster up" as they perform the song "General George." Challenge them to come up with a special drum signal to indicate different "troop" movements, such as line up, turn left, turn right, stop, or move forward. Allow students to take turns delivering signals as General Washington!

★A New Nation

Eleven states were part of the Union when Washington took office. Within a year, North Carolina and Vermont became the last two colonies of the original 13 to accept statehood. To give children a sense of what the country looked like around the time George Washington took office, have them assemble the puzzle pieces on page 20. To make the pieces easier to manipulate, you can enlarge the state shapes on a photocopier. To add durability, have children glue a photocopy of the page to oaktag before cutting out the shapes.

Children can work in small groups for this activity, to underscore the idea that the colonies had to work together and cooperate to form a new nation. Once students have completed their puzzles, display a map showing the United States today, and ask children to comment on how the country has changed since Washington's day.

★Don't Call Me King

Tell children that George Washington declined the suggestion that he become king, but accepted the office of president. To get children thinking about the difference between these roles, ask them to try the activity on page 21. Assign children partners and provide each pair with a copy of the reproducible. Partners should cut apart the fact strips on the bottom of the page, then try to sort them under the appropriate heading on the Venn diagram. Be sure students understand how the Venn diagram works and that shared characteristics should be placed in the area where the circles overlap. Encourage students to add more information to the different parts of the diagram if they are able to.

Discuss how children sorted the fact strips on the diagram. Help children understand that the United States set up a new type of government, and that the president was a new kind of leader—one voted into office by the people. Ask children for their ideas about why the United States decided against having a king.

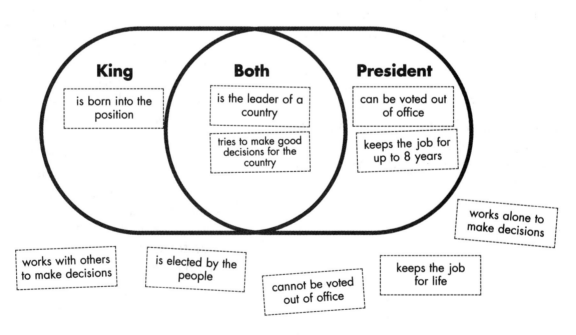

General George

Sing to the tune of "Yankee Doodle."

Washington, he was the one,
who led the Revolution.
To the cause of liberty
he made a contribution.

> *Chorus*
> General George, he won the war!
> General George, he beat 'em!
> General George, fought long and hard
> to gain our nation's freedom.

On Christmas Eve, he led his men
across the Delaware.
They reached the enemy at dawn
and caught them unaware.

> *Repeat Chorus*

In winter time at Valley Forge,
through cold and bitter weather,
Washington stuck with his men,
he held the troops together.

> *Repeat Chorus*

For eight long years, he led the troops,
our nation's brave defender,
till finally at Yorktown
the British did surrender.

> *Repeat Chorus*

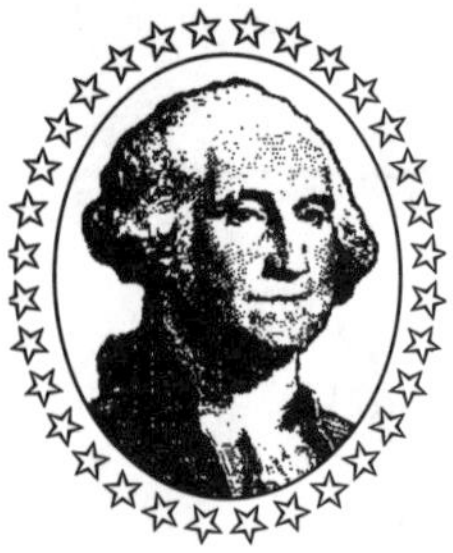

Name ____________________

A New Nation

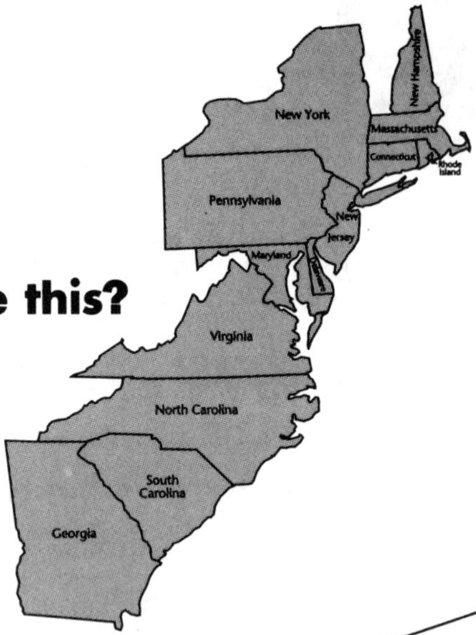
New York
New Hampshire
Massachusetts
Connecticut
Rhode Island
Pennsylvania
New Jersey
Maryland
Virginia
North Carolina
South Carolina
Georgia

Cut out the puzzle pieces.
Can you put them together to look like this?

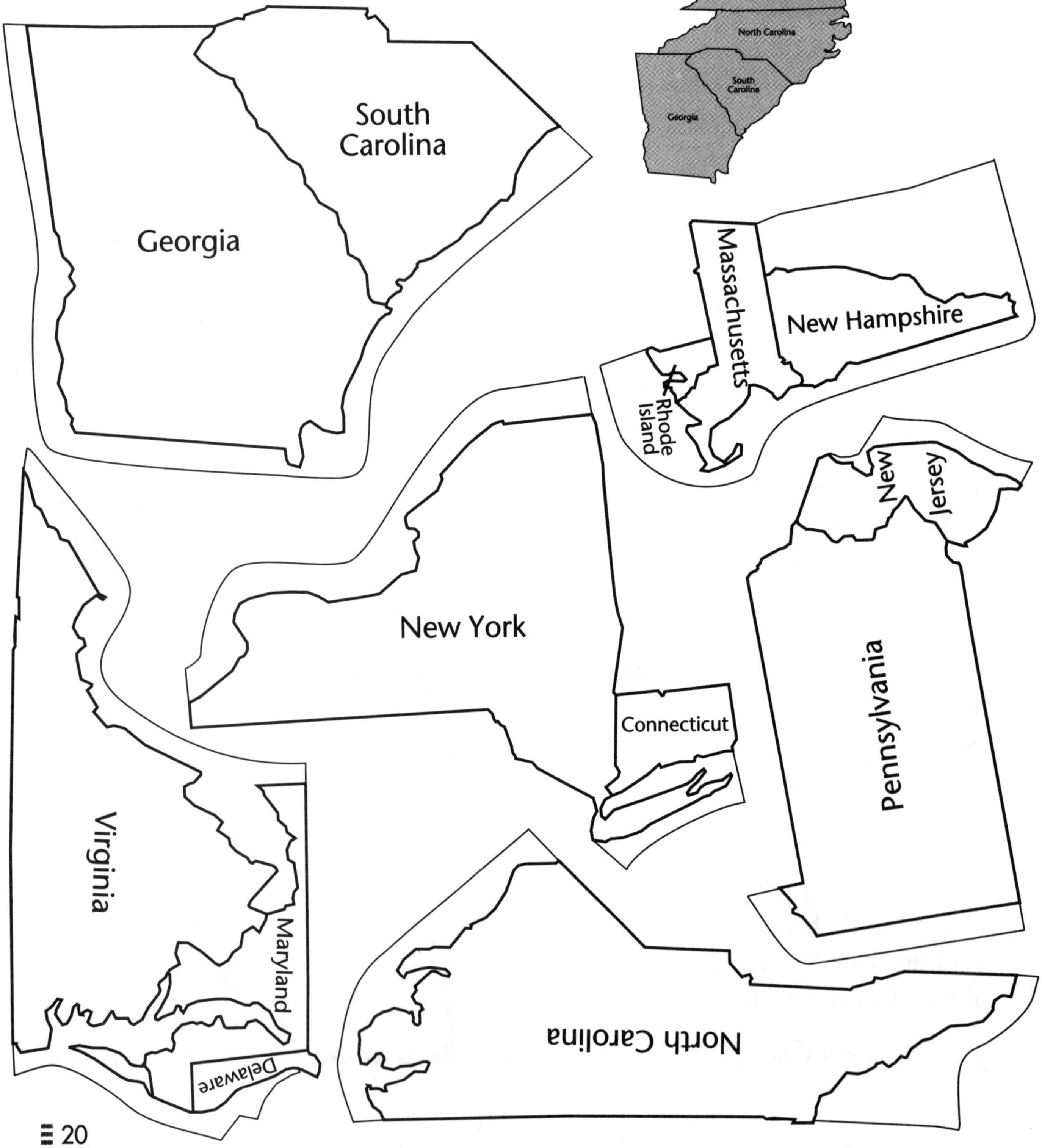
South Carolina
Georgia
Massachusetts
New Hampshire
Rhode Island
New York
New Jersey
Pennsylvania
Connecticut
Virginia
Maryland
Delaware
North Carolina

Don't Call Me King

Name _____

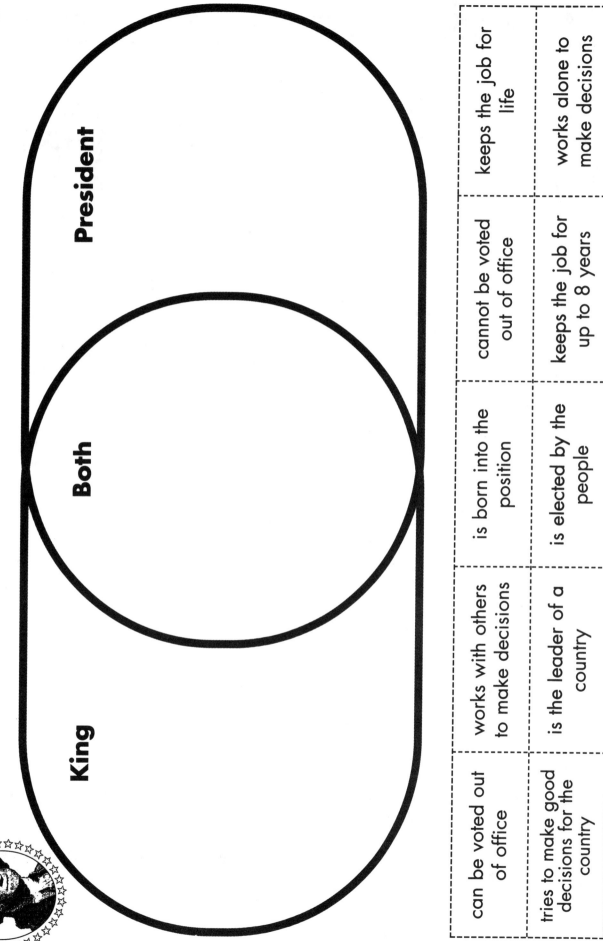

President

Both

King

keeps the job for life	cannot be voted out of office	is born into the position	works with others to make decisions
works alone to make decisions	keeps the job for up to 8 years	is elected by the people	is the leader of a country
			can be voted out of office
			tries to make good decisions for the country

CHAPTER 3

All About Abe

The Man and the Myth

As with George Washington, there are many famous stories about Abraham Lincoln. One of them tells about the time Dennis Hanks picked up his cousin, the infant Abe. After a few minutes of holding the bawling baby with skin "like red cherry pulp squeezed dry," Dennis handed Abe back to his mother, commenting, "Aunt, take him! He'll never come to much." The remark stands in ironic contrast to the near mythic stature achieved by our nation's 16th president.

A Frontier Family

Abraham Lincoln was born on February 12, 1809, the second child of Nancy and Thomas Lincoln. The one-room log cabin his family lived in was on Sinking Spring farm near Hodgenville, Kentucky. The Lincolns eked out a living in the Kentucky wilderness before moving to a new home site in Indiana.

Thomas Lincoln was a carpenter and farmer, and young Abe had a large share of chores to do around the homestead. He helped with the planting, plowing, and harvesting. By the age of eight, Abe was swinging an ax, which he used to clear acres of woods for farmland and to split trees for fences and firewood.

When Lincoln was nine years old, his mother died, plunging the family into sadness. About a year later, his father married a widow, Sarah Bush Johnston, who with her three children, brought new cheer into the gloomy home.

Learning By Littles

Describing his education, Lincoln said he went to school "by littles," attending when he could be spared from his chores. In total, he spent less than a year in a schoolhouse. But young Abraham was a voracious reader, and read any book he could get his hands on. Among his favorite books was a biography of George Washington, whom he deeply admired. Lincoln learned about the finer points of public speaking from a book called *Lessons in Elocution* that he found one day. Sometimes, he'd climb up on a stump and imitate local preachers and politicians to entertain his friends. His father taught Abe the art of storytelling, and people loved to listen to his jokes and yarns.

Early Career

At age 21, Lincoln moved with his family to Illinois. There, he struck out on his own and tried his hand at a number of jobs. He worked as a ferryboat captain and a store clerk. He found a partner and opened his own general store. The business failed and left Lincoln saddled with debt. He worked at a variety of jobs to pay off his creditors: farm hand, rail splitter, gristmill laborer, land surveyor. He even got a job as Post Master of New Salem, Illinois, where he lived for a time. Well-liked wherever he went, Lincoln built a reputation as a man of honesty and integrity.

Despite his modest beginnings and patchwork education, Lincoln was ambitious. In 1832, he ran for the state legislature and lost, only to run two years later and win. By his mid-20s, he held his first political office. Soon after, he earned his license to practice law. He found a partner and opened a law firm in Springfield, Illinois. Lincoln traveled around Illinois, handling cases for local farmers and for large corporations. In time, he became a successful and highly regarded lawyer.

Marriage and Family

In 1847, Abraham Lincoln married Mary Ann Todd, the daughter of a wealthy Kentucky banker. The Lincolns moved to a comfortable house in Springfield, where they lived for the next 17 years. Together they had four sons: Edward, Robert, William, and Thomas, called Tad. Ironically, Mary Todd's family had objected to the marriage, viewing Lincoln's "backwoods" upbringing and coarse manners with disdain. But Mary had seen potential in the young lawyer, and indeed, she was proven right. Four years after their marriage, he would be elected a Congressman, and 14 years after that, President of the United States.

LITERATURE LAUNCHERS

If You Grew Up with Abraham Lincoln by Ann McGovern (Scholastic, 1985) poses and answers questions about Lincoln's frontier childhood. *Abraham Lincoln* by Ingri and Edgar d'Aulaire (Doubleday, 1936) is a classic children's biography of Lincoln that also focuses on his childhood.

★What Do You Know About Abe?

As with George Washington, children will probably have prior knowledge about Abraham Lincoln. Activate this prior knowledge by creating a "KWL" chart for Lincoln. Divide a bulletin board into three columns, making the third one roughly twice as large as the first two. Label the first column, "What We Know About Lincoln"; label the second, "What We Want to Learn About Lincoln"; and the third, "What We've Learned About Lincoln." Invite children to record information and questions on the stovepipe hat pattern provided on page 26. Keep a supply of the patterns near the ongoing display, so children can add their questions and discoveries as you move through the unit. Compare what children learned with what they knew beforehand. Are there any discrepancies?

★From the Wilderness to the White House

Children can assemble a time line of the key events in Abraham Lincoln's life. You'll find patterns for making a time line in the shape of Lincoln's stovepipe hat on pages 27 and 28. Children can make the time line on their own, in groups, or as a class. To begin, make a photocopy of pages 27 and 28. (If you are making a class time line, you may want to enlarge the images to make a more prominent display.) Have children cut apart the fact strips on page 28, then arrange them in chronological order on the hat pattern on page 27, beginning with Lincoln's birth on the bottom and ending with his death at the top. Have students double-check the order of the dates before gluing the strips in place.

You may want to use the time line as the center of a bulletin board or wall display on Abraham Lincoln's life. Children can add information, quotations, stories, and other materials to the display as they learn more about Lincoln.

★A Life in Pictures

Abraham Lincoln was the most photographed man of his time. Children can look at some of these powerful images as they make a mini-photobiography of Lincoln using reproducible pages 29–31. Begin by making a double-sided photocopy of the pages for each child, being careful not to invert the photos on the reverse side of the page. To make the book, follow these directions:

☆ Place the page with the photographs on the desk, with panels A and B facing up.

☆ Cut along the solid line to separate panel A from panel B.

☆ Lay panel B on top of panel A so that the pages are in the correct order.

☆ Fold the stacked panels along the dashed line and staple along the left edge to secure the pages.

☆ Cut apart the caption boxes on page 31.

☆ Find the photo in the book that each caption tells about. Glue the captions under the correct photos to complete the album.

 Lincoln Logs

Lincoln's frontier boyhood is legendary, and there are many wonderful picture books that describe it. Make some of these books available to children (see Literature Launchers and Additional Resources on page 56). Then ask students to go on a fact-hunt and track down information about Lincoln's boyhood. Provide each child with a copy of reproducible page 32. Students can write some of the facts they discover on the log patterns. Provide children with half-pint milk cartons (rinsed and dried), paints, crayons, scissors, and glue. Have children follow these simple directions to make mini-models of Lincoln's boyhood home to display their research:

☆ Paint the carton a dark color, such as brown. Let it dry.

☆ Color the roof pieces. Cut them out.

☆ Paste or staple the roof pieces to the top of the carton.

☆ After writing facts on the logs, color them and cut them out.

☆ Paste the logs on the milk carton so that it resembles a cabin.

Set up a table-top resource center where children can display their model log cabins. Allow time for children to share and compare the facts they've discovered.

★ The Joke's On You

Lincoln was known for his ready sense of humor. When he was young, he played a practical joke on his stepmother. As a listening activity, read aloud to children the famous "Muddy Foot Joke" on this page. Then distribute a copy of page 33 to each child. Ask students to cut out the footprints and paste them in the correct order to illustrate the sequence of events in the story. As

a math extension, help students use rulers or tape measures to mark off a height of 6 feet, 4 inches on a wall. Ask students to compare Lincoln's height with their own. How much taller was he?

The Muddy Foot Joke

Abe Lincoln was "a tall spider of a boy," people used to say. By the time he was a young man, Abe stood 6'4" tall in his stocking feet. His stepmother, Sarah Lincoln, liked to joke about his height. "Pretty soon you'll have to duck your head to fit inside the house," she would tease Abe. "Now, you better keep your head washed, or you'll be leaving dirt on my nice clean ceiling."

Sarah Lincoln's joke made Abe laugh. It also gave him an idea for a joke he could play on *her*. One day, he asked some children to walk barefoot through a big muddy puddle. Then, when his stepmother was out of the house, he brought the children inside.

Abe wasn't just big. He was also strong. He picked the children up one by one and turned them upside down. Then he "walked" the children across the ceiling. They left their muddy footprints all over the clean white ceiling!

When Abe's stepmother came home, she looked up in surprise. Who in the world had been walking on her ceiling? Then a smile swept across her face. "Why, Abraham Lincoln, I ought to spank you," she said, laughing. Sarah and her stepson had a good chuckle over the joke as Abe got a bucket of whitewash and painted the ceiling over, good as new.

What Do You Know About Abe?

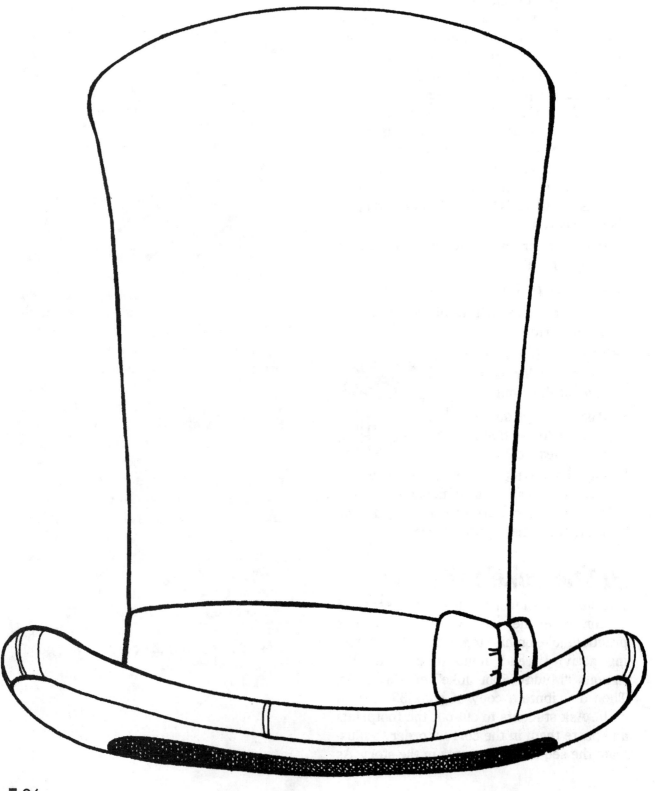

Name _____

From the Wilderness to the White House

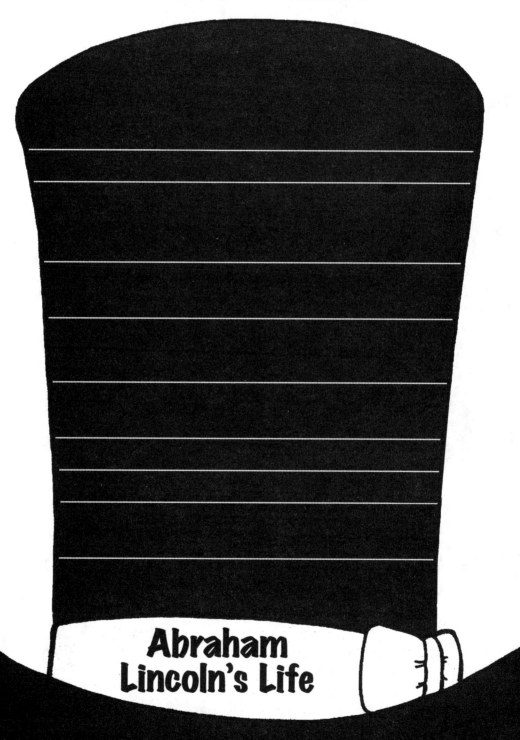

Abraham Lincoln's Life

From the Wilderness to the White House

1809 Abe Lincoln is born on February 12 in a log cabin in Kentucky.

1863 Lincoln signs the Emancipation Proclamation. It frees slaves in the rebelling southern states.

1834 Lincoln serves in the state government of Illinois.

1864 Lincoln is reelected President.

1861 The South leaves the Union, and the Civil War begins.

1842 Lincoln marries Mary Todd.

1860 Lincoln is elected the 16th President of the United States.

1846 Lincoln becomes a U.S. Congressman.

1836 Lincoln becomes a lawyer.

1865 The Civil War ends. Soon after, Lincoln is shot. He dies on April 15.

Abe Lincoln: A Life in Pictures

Panel A

2

7

Panel B

4

5

Name _____

Abraham Lincoln: A Life in Pictures

These sentences go with the pictures in your Abe Lincoln book. Cut out the sentences. Paste them under the correct pictures.

Lincoln worked at many jobs before he became President. For a time, he owned this store in New Salem, Illinois.

Lincoln was killed shortly after the Civil War ended. A man shot Lincoln while he was watching a play in this theater.

This is what Lincoln looked like when he was elected President. Do you see his thick whiskers? He was the first U.S. President to have a beard.

Lincoln led the country through the Civil War. Here, he meets with army leaders. Do you see his famous hat?

Lincoln loved to read and play with his sons. Here, he is with his son Tad. The boys were the first children ever to live in the White House.

Lincoln was born in a log cabin that looked like this. It was in Kentucky.

When he was 33 years old, Lincoln married Mary Todd. They had four sons.

Lincoln Logs

Find out about Abe Lincoln as a boy. Write some facts about his boyhood on the log shapes. Cut out the log shapes and roof pieces. Glue them to a milk carton to make a model of Lincoln's boyhood home.

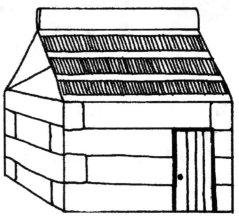

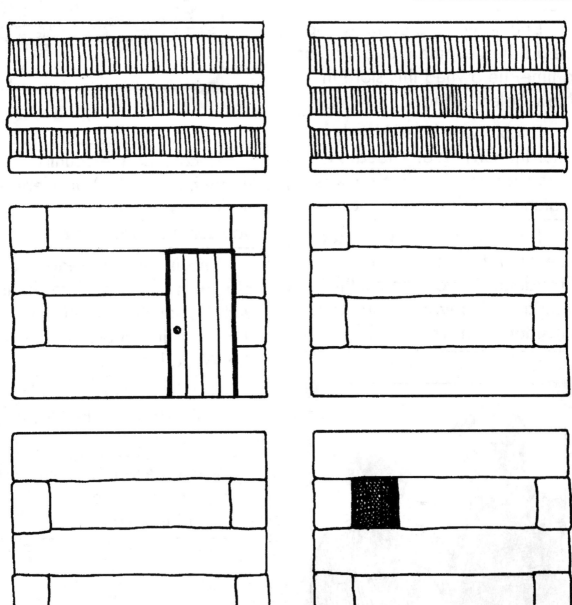

Name _____

The Joke's on You

Abe Lincoln once played a joke on his stepmother. These footprints tell the story. But they are out of order. Cut out the prints. Paste them in the right order on another paper. Retell the story about Abe's joke to a friend or someone at home.

Abe's stepmother is surprised. There are muddy footprints all over her ceiling!

Abe's stepmother teases him because he is tall. This gives Abe an idea for a joke.

Abe asks some children to step in a muddy puddle. He carries them into his house.

Abe paints the ceiling white again. He and his stepmother laugh about the joke.

Abe holds the children upside down. He "walks" them across the ceiling.

CHAPTER 4

President of a Divided Nation

Conflicts Over Slavery

Lincoln took his political career to the national level in 1847, with his election to the U.S. House of Representatives. At that time, conflicts between the North and South over the issue of slavery were intensifying. While Lincoln believed slavery was morally wrong, he did not come out strongly against it at this point.

In 1854, however, Congress passed the Kansas-Nebraska Act. This law allowed states entering the Union to decide for themselves whether they would join as slave or free states. Lincoln believed this measure encouraged the growth, rather than the decline, of slavery in America, and it alarmed him greatly.

A Path to the Presidency

In 1858, Lincoln ran against the Illinois Senator, Stephen A. Douglas, who had initiated the Kansas-Nebraska Act. During the Senate campaign, Lincoln and Douglas debated the issue of slavery. Lincoln spoke forcefully and eloquently against the evils of the institution. Although Lincoln lost the election, the debates gained him national recognition. Two years later, he was nominated as the Republican presidential candidate and won the office. On March 4, 1861, Abraham Lincoln was inaugurated as the sixteenth president of the United States. He was 52 years old.

The South Secedes

Lincoln's election put the South in an uproar. Since slave labor supported the large plantations of the agricultural South, white southerners saw Lincoln's election as a threat to their economy and way of life. Eleven southern states withdrew from the Union to form a new nation: The Confederate States of America. Jefferson Davis, a Senator from Mississippi, became the Confederacy's president. And on April 12, 1861—just over a month after Lincoln's inauguration—civil war broke out between the North and South.

Equality for All

The Civil War dragged on for four long years. Initially, Lincoln's primary objective was to reunite the nation; he was even willing to allow slavery to continue in the South in order to restore the Union. But in time, his views changed, and he saw the dismantling of slavery as a political and moral imperative. On New Year's Day in 1863, Abraham Lincoln issued the Emancipation Proclamation. While the proclamation freed slaves only in the rebelling southern states, it paved the way for the Thirteenth Amendment, passed in 1865, which banned slavery in all parts of the United States.

The Gettysburg Address

In July of 1863, the Battle of Gettysburg was fought. This big Union victory turned the war in the North's favor, but both sides paid an enormous toll: at the end of the three-day battle, nearly 50,000 men lay dead.

Lincoln delivered a two-minute speech praising the sacrifices of the soldiers who had died so that democracy might live, and "government of the people, by the people, and for the people, shall not perish from this earth." Little attention was paid to his remarks at the time, but Lincoln's Gettysburg Address became one of the most famous speeches in U.S. history.

Lincoln's Home Life

In addition to the strain of war, Lincoln had family problems to contend with. In 1862, the Lincolns' son Willie died from a fever. Edward had died earlier in 1850 at the age of four. Lincoln doted on his children, and Willie's death devastated both him and his wife. These events, along with the death and suffering of the Civil War, sank Lincoln into a despair than many said became etched on his face.

Peace Arrives

In 1864 Lincoln was elected to a second term. Shortly thereafter, the Southern General Robert E. Lee surrendered, and the bloody war ended. In his second inaugural address Lincoln urged the nation to work toward healing the wounds that divided it. "With malice toward none, with charity for all; . . . let us strive on to finish the work we are in; to bind up the nation's wounds; ...to do all which may achieve and cherish a just, and a lasting, peace. . . ."

A Fateful Night

For many years there had been threats on Lincoln's life. And on the night of April 14, 1865, a southern patriot named John Wilkes Booth succeeded in shooting Lincoln in the back of the head at the Ford Theater. Lincoln died the next morning, on April 15, 1865. He was 56 years old. Standing by the bedside, his Secretary of War, Edwin M. Stanton, said quietly, "Now he belongs to the ages."

LITERATURE LAUNCHERS

Abraham Lincoln: President of a Divided Country by Carol Greene (Childrens Press, 1989) offers young readers an overview of the Lincoln presidency. *Abe Lincoln and the End of Slavery* by Russell Shorto provides a straightforward explanation of the complicated issue of slavery, and Lincoln's beliefs about the institution.

★ A Word of Advice

When Lincoln was running for president in 1860, an 11-year-old girl named Grace Bedell sent him a letter advising him to grow a beard. On page 38, you'll find an excerpt from this letter. Grace Bedell's letter tickled Lincoln, and he liked to pull it out to show others. Read aloud Grace's letter to the class. Then ask the children to study the two pictures to see if Lincoln took her advice. (He grew whiskers by the time he took office in 1861.)

Ask students if they have any advice to offer the current President, perhaps about how to handle a national problem or win the public's support. Children can write their thoughts in a letter, and send it to the White House at the address below. If students write individual letters, the White House will send back a photo of the President and a postcard message; if students write a collective letter, your class will be sent a letter and a teaching packet that includes a poster.

The President
The White House
1600 Pennsylvania Avenue
Washington, DC 20500

★ Torn in Two

Provide children with background information about the Civil War. You may want to read aloud parts of the book *If You Lived at the Time of the Civil War* by Kay Moore (Scholastic, 1994), which offers a straightforward explanation of the issues behind the war. Explain the terms "Union" and "Confederate" as they relate to the northern and southern states at this period in U.S. history.

Once children have a basic understanding of the Civil War, distribute reproducible page 39. This map shows which states withdrew from the Union after Lincoln was elected President. Ask children to think about questions such as the following:

☆ Why did Lincoln think it was worth fighting to keep the nation together?

☆ Do you agree with him that it was important? Why or why not?

☆ What might America be like today if the country had split apart?

★ Divided We Fall

As a follow-up to the map activity, share with children this quote from Lincoln and ask for ideas about its meaning:

A house divided against itself cannot stand. I believe this government cannot endure, permanently half-slave and half-free. I do not expect the union to be dissolved—I do not expect the house to fall—but I do expect it will cease to be divided. It will become all one thing, or all the other.

Students can try this simple activity, which offers a visual echo of Lincoln's famous words:

☆ Make an extra copy of the map on page 39.

☆ Gather a bunch of small building blocks (roughly 2" × 2"). Cut out the box that contains the map. Then cut it into pieces that match the size of the building blocks.

☆ Tape the map squares to the blocks (one square per block).

☆ Reassemble the map by stacking up the blocks.

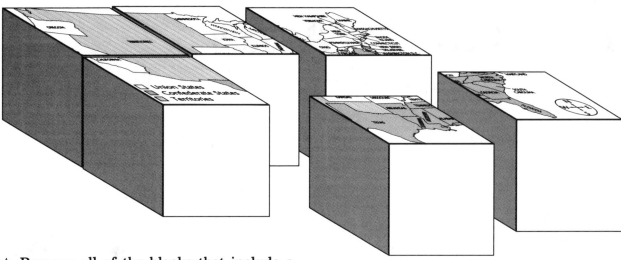

☆ Remove all of the blocks that include a piece of the map that is shaded gray, to simulate the secession of the southern states from the Union. What happens to the rest of the country?

★ "To Meet Mr. Lincoln"

In the poem on this page, the child narrator imagines meeting Abraham Lincoln. Read aloud the poem. You may want to use it as a discussion starter about the things that troubled Mr. Lincoln when he was president. Ask children what they think made him look "worn and sad-eyed" *(the existence of slavery in the United States, the division of the country into two parts, the loss of lives in the Civil War, the personal loss of his own two sons).* Follow up by distributing to children a copy of page 40, which asks children to imagine what they would say to Mr. Lincoln if they could meet him.

Remind children that Lincoln had the courage to try to change what was wrong with the country, to fix the things that saddened him, such as slavery and the division of the Union. Ask children to think about things about our country today that make them sad. What can be done to change these things? What can children do to help? Suggest that children write their thoughts in their journals.

To Meet Mr. Lincoln
If I lived at the time
That Mr. Lincoln did,
And I met Mr. Lincoln
With his stovepipe lid
And his coalblack cape
And his thundercloud beard,
And worn and sad-eyed
he appeared:
"Don't worry, Mr. Lincoln,"
I'd reach up and pat his hand,
"We've got a fine President
For this land;
"And the Union will be saved,
And the slaves will go free;
And you will live forever
In our nation's memory."

—Eve Merriam

A Word of Advice

Hon A B Lincoln...

Oct. 15, 1860

Dear Sir

....I am a little girl only eleven years old, but want you should be President of the United States very much so I hope you wont think me very bold to write to such a great man as you are. Have you any little girls about as large as I am if so give them my love and tell her to write to me if you cannot answer this letter. I have got 4 brother's and part of them will vote for you any way and if you let your whiskers grow I will try and get the rest of them to vote for you you would look a great deal better for your face is so thin. All the ladies like whiskers and they would tease their husband's to vote for you and then you would be President. My father is a going to vote for you and if I was a man I would vote for you to but I will try and get every one to vote for you that I can...

I must not write any more answer this letter right off Good bye

Grace Bedell

Name _____

Torn in Two

This map shows what happened when Lincoln became President. Some states left the Union. They became the Confederate States.

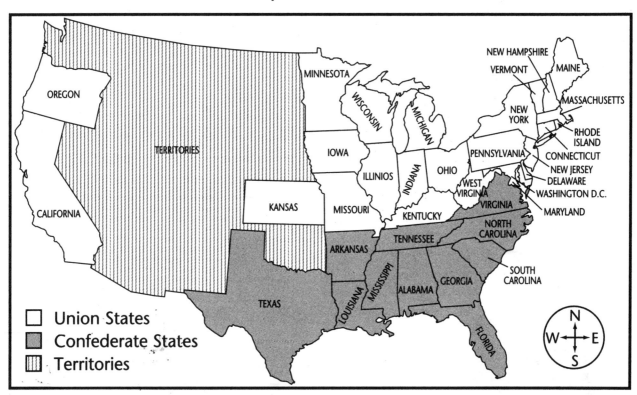

Union States
Confederate States
Territories

Use the map to answer the questions.

1. Did Texas stay in the Union? _____ Did Indiana? _____

2. Name two states on the west coast that were part of the Union.

_____

3. How many Confederate states were there? _____

In what part of the country were these states? _____

4. Is your state on this map? _____ If so, what side was it on in the

Civil War?_____

Name _____

"To Meet Mr. Lincoln"

If I lived at the time
That Mr. Lincoln did,
And I met Mr. Lincoln
With his stovepipe lid....

Imagine you did meet Mr. Lincoln.
What would you like to ask him or say to him?

**Draw a picture of you talking to Mr. Lincoln in the box.
Then write what you'd say to him in the speech balloon.**

CHAPTER 5

Heading Into History

Honors Galore

George Washington and Abraham Lincoln are two of our greatest and most admired Presidents. Each year, millions of people visit the Lincoln Memorial and the Washington Monument in the nation's capital. The faces of both men are immortalized in stone at Mt. Rushmore Memorial in South Dakota which you can see on the poster. Hundreds of towns, rivers, bridges, schools, and streets are also named after these Presidents. Coins, bills, and postage stamps bear their portraits. Their birthdays are celebrated as a national holiday on President's Day in February.

Moving Beyond the Myths

In some ways, George Washington and Abraham Lincoln have become part of our nation's mythology. There are many stories about each—some true, some not—that idealize their characters. Just what is it that made these men so great? What can children learn from our most famous Presidents?

Born to Lead

Each man had a particular gift for leadership, and each helped navigate the nation through crucial periods in its history. Both men are also admired for their character as much as for their accomplishments.

Despite incredible obstacles and setbacks, Washington remained committed to the fight for independence during the American Revolution. Later, he overcame his own feelings of insecurity and fears of failure to become the nation's first President—not out of ambition, but out of a deep sense of duty to his country.

Lincoln, too, demonstrated a nobility of character. His difficult decisions about the issue of slavery and the Civil War made him unpopular—even hated—but he stuck by them. A peace-loving man, Lincoln was sickened and saddened by the fighting, but he continued the war because he believed it was necessary for the good of the country. In spite of the bitterness of the struggle, Lincoln remained compassionate toward those suffering on both sides.

LITERATURE LAUNCHERS

I Did It with My Hatchet by Robert Quackenbush (Pippin, 1989) explores the myths and realities of George Washington's life; *True Stories About Abraham Lincoln* by Ruth Belov Gross (Lothrop, 1989) tackles the same topic for our 16th president. *The Buck Stops Here* by Alice Provensen (Harper, 1990) is a rhymed tribute to all our nation's presidents, and it offers a nice way to celebrate the accomplishments of both Washington and Lincoln.

STUDENT ACTIVITIES

⭐Fact or Fiction?

Children can make a flap book that explores popular stories about George Washington and Abraham Lincoln. Make a double-sided photocopy of pages 45–46 for each child, being careful not to invert the text on the back. Share these directions with students for making and using the book:

☆ Position the page so that the side with the pictures on it faces up. Fold the page in half along the dashed line.

☆ Cut along the solid lines on the front of the folded side.

☆ Read the front of each flap and guess whether or not it's true. Lift the flap to find out if it's fact or fiction.

After reading the flap book, ask students to offer their ideas about why people may have passed along (and, in some cases, invented!) these stories about George Washington and Abraham Lincoln. Which ones are just interesting stories? Which tell something about the characters of the two men?

Extend the discussion to the topic of character as it relates to leadership. What qualities do children think it takes to be a good leader? As a class, brainstorm a list of these characteristics, and write them on the chalkboard or chart paper. Then ask students which of these characteristics Washington and Lincoln showed. Challenge students to cite specific examples of how Washington and Lincoln demonstrated these characteristics.

⭐Dreaming of George and Abe

Children may enjoy performing the play on pages 47–51. This play encourages a focus on the contributions of Washington and Lincoln rather than just the popular stories about these men. Students can follow up their performance by writing the play that the character Connie might have written after George and Abe paid her a visit.

⭐On the Way to the White House

On pages 52–55, you'll find a gameboard and cards for a trivia game focusing on Washington and Lincoln. The object of the game is to advance to the White House by correctly identifying whether a factual statement applies to Washington or Lincoln. The game is an excellent way to review and reinforce what children have learned about each President. To set up and play the game, follow these directions:

Setting Up the Game

1. Divide the class into groups of 2 or 4.

2. Provide each group with a photocopy of pages 52–53. Have students tape the pages together, side-by-side, making sure that the two halves of the gameboard are properly aligned.

3. Provide groups with a photocopy of pages 54–55. Cut apart the Fact Cards from the Bonus Cards on page 55. Glue each sheet of Fact Cards to a sheet of the same color construction paper. Glue the sheet of Bonus Cards to a different colored sheet of construction paper. Cut all the cards apart along the dashed lines.

4. Separate the cards into Fact and Bonus groups, mix each group up, and place them face down on the gameboard where indicated. (You may want to laminate the gameboard and fact cards for durability.)

5. Children can play either one-on-one or team against team. Provide one child or team with a penny (Lincoln) and the other with a quarter (Washington) to use as playing pieces.

6. The child or team representing Lincoln should place the penny on the square nearest Lincoln's Kentucky log cabin. The child or team representing Washington should place the quarter on the square nearest Washington's boyhood home, Ferry Farm, in Virginia.

Rules for Playing:

1. Roll a die to see who goes first.

2. Depending on who goes first, the opposing player or team should draw a Fact Card from the top of the deck and read it aloud. The player whose turn it is needs to guess whether the fact is true for Lincoln or Washington. If she or he answers correctly, the player rolls the die and moves forward the number of spaces indicated. If the player answers incorrectly, he or she must stay put.

3. When it is the next player's turn, his or her opponent should draw a Fact Card from the pile and read it aloud. Again, the player must guess if the statement applies to Washington or Lincoln, then roll the die and move forward if the answer is correct. Play should continue in this way, with each player taking a turn and trying to advance toward the White House. If children run out of Fact Cards during the course of the game, reshuffle and use them again.

4. If players land on a square marked "Skip a Turn," they must do just that. If players land on a square marked "Roll Again," they may roll again and move the indicated number of spaces *without* having to answer another question. If they land on a square marked "Bonus," their opponent should draw a card from the Bonus Card stack and read the question. If students can answer the question correctly, they get to advance the same number of squares that they last rolled. If they answer incorrectly, they stay where they are and it becomes their opponents' turn.

5. The winner is the first person to reach the White House.

(Note: You may want to point out to children that the White House was not yet constructed during Washington's presidency, but he was involved in the planning of the nation's capital city.)

Happy Birthday, Mr. President!

Throw a Presidents' Day birthday party to culminate your study of George Washington and Abraham Lincoln. Following are some suggestions for the celebration. Encourage students to contribute their ideas to the party planning:

☆ **Decorations:** Red, white, and blue streamers would make festive decorations for a Presidents' Day celebration. Alternatively, have children make paper chains using red, white, and blue construction paper. Hang these as garlands around the room. Lumps of clay in small paper cups can secure small American flags, which can then be displayed around the room. Encourage children to dress in patriotic colors on the assigned day. Children may even want to make stovepipe or tri-cornered hats to wear in honor of Lincoln and Washington. (For directions to make the hats, see prop list from the play on page 47.)

☆ **Food:** Enlist children's help to bake and decorate a sheet cake that resembles the U.S. flag (use an oblong 13" × 9" × 2" cake pan). Tint some vanilla frosting red and some blue to make the stripes and blue background for the stars. Ask students to calculate how old George Washington and Abraham Lincoln would be today before singing happy birthday and blowing out the candles on the cake. Encourage students to think of other red-white-and-blue foods you might serve for the occasion, for example vanilla yogurt parfaits made with strawberries and blueberries.

☆ **Music:** Play music with patriotic themes, such as "Yankee Doodle" (sung in Washington's day) or "Battle Hymn of the Republic" (sung in Lincoln's day). Children may enjoy performing the song "General George" (see page 19). They can also chant, or make up a tune for, the following cheer. It is a traditional salute to George Washington, but students can repeat it using Lincoln's name as well:

> Fill the glasses to the brink,
> To Washington's health we'll drink,
> 'Tis his birthday!
> Glorious deeds he has done,
> By him our cause is won,
> Long live great Washington!

☆ **Activities:** Invite guests into your classroom for a performance of the play "Dreaming of George and Abe" (see page 47), or a "mustering up" demonstration (see page 17). Hold a joke-swapping session in honor of Abe Lincoln's sense of humor. Before the celebration, invite children to research colonial and frontier games to play at the party. (Two good sources for these games are *If You Grew Up with George Washington* and *If You Grew Up with Abraham Lincoln*; see Additional Resources on page 56.)

☆ **Reflections:** Display the poem "President's Day" by Myra Cohn Livingston on the poster bound into the center of this book. Allow time for children to reflect about what made George Washington and Abraham Lincoln so great. Prior to the event, children may wish to write their own poems honoring these men, which they then can share as a tribute to Washington and Lincoln during the birthday celebration.

Fact or Fiction?

When he was little, George Washington cut down a cherry tree with his hatchet. When his father asked him about the tree, George said, "I cannot tell a lie. I did it with my hatchet."

Fact or Fiction?

George Washington had wooden teeth. They gave him a lot of pain during his life.

Fact or Fiction?

Abraham Lincoln worked in a store when he was a young man. Once, a woman paid him 6 cents too much. After work, Lincoln walked three miles to the woman's house to return the money.

Fact or Fiction?

Abraham Lincoln was born in a one-room log cabin. He was very poor when he was growing up.

False. Washington may have had a hatchet when he was little, but there's no proof he ever cut down a cherry tree with it.

False. Washington did have fake teeth, but they were not made of wood. They were made from the teeth of a hippo. Sometimes these teeth did hurt him though.

True. After Lincoln returned the money to the woman, he got the nickname "Honest Abe" in his hometown.

True and False. Lincoln was born in a log cabin, and his family never had much money. But he wasn't terribly poor. Many frontier families lived off the land the way the Lincolns did.

Name _____

Dreaming of George and Abe

by Jim Halverson and Carol Pugliano

CHARACTERS:
Lisa
Marci
Connie
Andrew
George Washington
Abraham Lincoln

PROPS:
- two George Washington tri-cornered hats, each cut from three construction paper strips stapled together with cotton batting glued on from behind to simulate white wigs
- two Abraham Lincoln hats consisting of top-hat shapes cut from black construction paper and stapled to headbands sized to fit students heads.

★ACT 1   *A classroom.*

[The children enter.]

LISA: So what are you going to do next Monday?

MARCI: Go to school, of course. What a silly question!

CONNIE: Marci, we don't have school on Monday, remember? It's Presidents' Day.

MARCI: Oh right. I forgot.

ANDREW: I can't wait! It will be great to have an extra day to sleep late and play all day!

MARCI: Is that why we have Presidents' Day?

LISA: No. Presidents' Day celebrates the birthdays of our two most famous Presidents, George Washington and Abraham Lincoln.

CONNIE: That's right. And I've been thinking of something special we can do. Let's put on a Presidents' Day play.

LISA: That's a great idea! I'll be Abraham Lincoln.

ANDREW: And I'll be George Washington.

MARCI: What can I be?

CONNIE: You can be the Narrator.

LISA: What will you be, Connie?

CONNIE: The director, of course!

[They exit.]

★ACT 2   Connie's house.

[The kids are sitting around. They seem tired. Lisa is wearing a Lincoln hat and Andrew is wearing a Washington hat.]

MARCI: Connie, we've been working on this play for hours. I'm getting tired.

ANDREW: Can't we take a break?

CONNIE: We want this play to be perfect don't we?

ALL: [tiredly] Well,...but....

CONNIE: Then, let's try it again from the beginning. Washington, you stand there. And Lincoln, you go there. Marci, stand up front and begin.

Marci: Welcome to our little play
all about Presidents' Day.
Our play is short and fun to see.
We'll start with George and the
cherry tree.

[Marci steps back and Andrew, as George, steps forward.]

ANDREW: Once I got a brand new ax.
I loved it so, I could not relax.
I chopped at all that I could see
including my father's cherry tree.
When my dad asked me if I knew
who chopped the tree, what could I do?
I said, Dad, I cannot tell a lie—
I chopped the tree, I don't know why.

CONNIE: Excellent! Now you go back to your place.

ANDREW: Connie, are you sure that's why we celebrate George Washington's birthday? Just because he told the truth about a cherry tree?

CONNIE: Of course!

ANDREW: I guess so. But didn't he do anything better than just chop a tree down? I mean the whole country celebrates his birthday!

CONNIE: Never mind. Okay, Abraham Lincoln, you're up next.

[Lisa steps forward.]

LISA: When I was young, I was very poor.
I had no money, that's for sure.
I lived in a house that was made of logs.
We didn't have any cats or dogs.

CONNIE: Perfect.

LISA: Connie, this is silly! So, Lincoln was poor. Is that why we celebrate his birthday? And who cares if he didn't have any cats or dogs?

MARCI: Lisa is right. Being poor doesn't seem like much of a reason for Lincoln to be so famous.

CONNIE: Will you trust me? The play will be great. *[yawns]* You know, I'm kind of tired myself. I think I'll just lie down for a minute. Let me borrow your hat. It will help me think better while I rest.

[Connie puts on Lisa's Abraham Lincoln hat and lies down.]

ANDREW: *[lying down]* That's the best idea I've heard all day!

LISA: Sounds good to me.

MARCI: Me, too!

[They also lie down and all are soon asleep. Washington and Lincoln enter. They are more formally dressed than the children.]

WASHINGTON: So, Mr. Lincoln, what do you think of the play?

LINCOLN: Well, Mr. Washington, it's cute. But I think Connie needs more information.

WASHINGTON: I agree. Let's talk to her.

[Washington and Lincoln go over to Connie who is asleep. Lincoln gently taps her.]

LINCOLN: Hello, Connie.

[Connie screams and stands up quickly. She and Abe are face to face. She touches her hat and Abe touches his. She lifts her hat off, Abe lifts his. She puts her hat back on, so does Abe.]

CONNIE: AHHH!!! Who are you?

LINCOLN: I'm Abraham Lincoln. I'd like you to meet George Washington.

WASHINGTON: *[shaking Connie's hand]* How do you do?

CONNIE: *[surprised]* Hello. What are you doing here?

WASHINGTON: We heard about your play. We think you should know a little bit more about us before you go on.

CONNIE: You do?

LINCOLN: Yes. It's true that George Washington here was a very honest man. But he did many other wonderful things too.

CONNIE: Like what?

LINCOLN: Well, Mr. Washington helped to make our country free. He also became the very first President of the United States. He's known as the Father of Our Country.

WASHINGTON: Well, thank you, Mr. Lincoln, my good man.

LINCOLN: You're welcome. I've always been a big fan of yours.

WASHINGTON: Well, thank you. But, Mr. Lincoln, you were a pretty great man yourself.

CONNIE: He was? What did he do?

WASHINGTON: Mr. Lincoln believed that all people should be treated equally, no matter what color their skin was. He helped to free the slaves.

CONNIE: Wow. That is great!

LINCOLN: Well, we don't mean to brag. We just want you to put on a play that really helps other children learn about why they're celebrating our day.

WASHINGTON: Yes. The stories you tell in your play are fun, but they're not all that children should know.

CONNIE: Well, thanks for your help, Mr. Washington and Mr. Lincoln.

LINCOLN: You're welcome. Now why don't you finish your nap? *[He takes off his hat.]*

WASHINGTON: Yes, great playwrights need their rest. Goodbye!

[They exit. Lincoln leaves his hat behind.]

CONNIE: *[going back to sleep]* Goodbye.

[The other children stir and wake up.]

MARCI: What a great nap!

ANDREW: I feel much better.

LISA: Connie, wake up! Let's get back to work.

CONNIE: Okay, Mr. Washington. Huh? Oh, you missed it! George Washington and Abraham Lincoln were just here!

ANDREW: Come on! Like we believe you.

LISA: You must have been dreaming!

CONNIE: But it was so real. They told me all about themselves. Now I know what terrific men they really were. I'm going to rewrite the play to tell about their great deeds!

MARCI: Wow! What was it like to talk with them?

CONNIE: It was great. Too bad it was just a dream... *[She sees Abe's hat and picks it up]* ....or was it?....

THE END

On the Way to

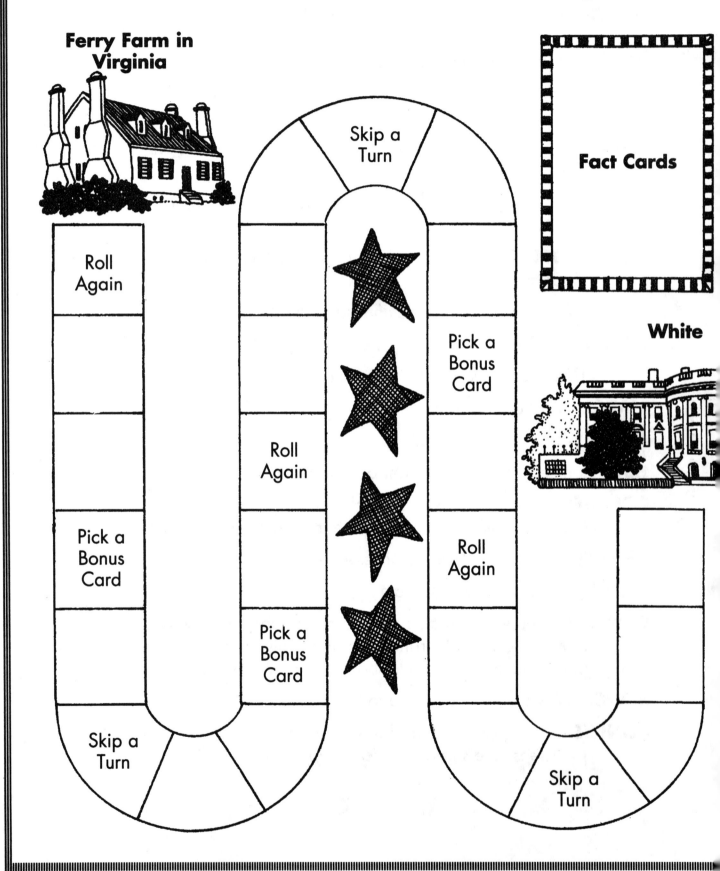

Ferry Farm in Virginia

Fact Cards

White

Roll Again

Skip a Turn

Pick a Bonus Card

Roll Again

Pick a Bonus Card

Roll Again

Skip a Turn

Pick a Bonus Card

Roll Again

Skip a Turn

the White House

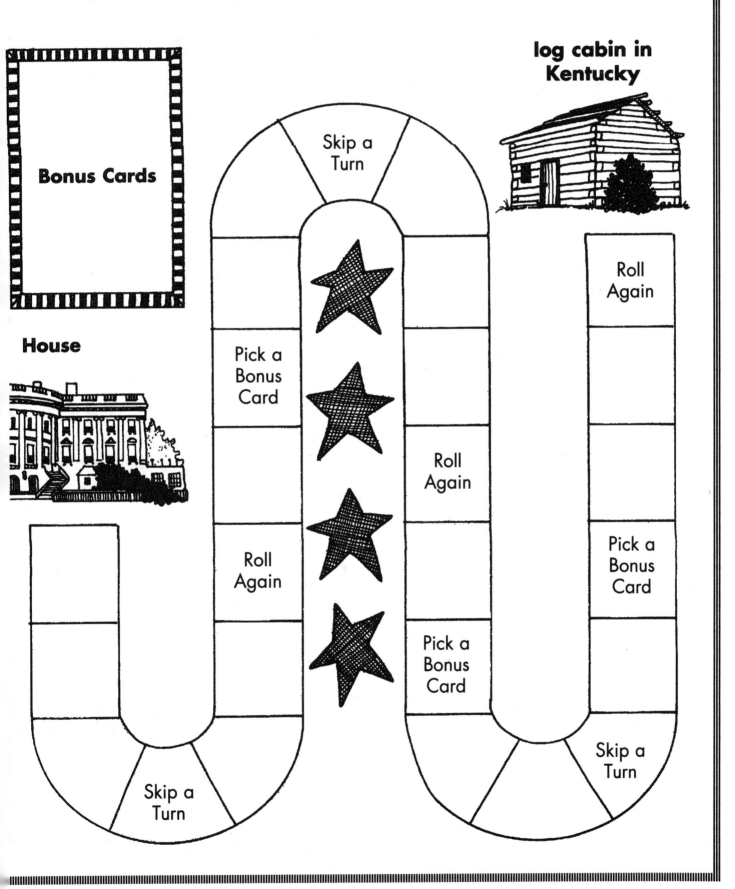

Bonus Cards

House

log cabin in Kentucky

Skip a Turn

Pick a Bonus Card

Roll Again

Skip a Turn

Roll Again

Pick a Bonus Card

Roll Again

Pick a Bonus Card

Skip a Turn

? FACT CARD ?

I was the first President of the United States.

(WASHINGTON)

? FACT CARD ?

When I grew up, the United States was not a nation yet.

(WASHINGTON)

? FACT CARD ?

There were only 11 states when I became President.

(WASHINGTON)

? FACT CARD ?

I led the troops during the American Revolution.

(WASHINGTON)

? FACT CARD ?

I helped write the United States Constitution.

(WASHINGTON)

? FACT CARD ?

I went to school for less than one year during my life.

(LINCOLN)

? FACT CARD ?

I was a surveyor when I was young. That means I measured land.

(WASHINGTON)

? FACT CARD ?

I am called "The Father of My Country."

(WASHINGTON)

? FACT CARD ?

I was born in the year 1809.

(LINCOLN)

? FACT CARD ?

I had false teeth made from a hippo's teeth.

(WASHINGTON)

? FACT CARD ?

Today, people visit my home, Mt. Vernon, in Virginia.

(WASHINGTON)

? FACT CARD ?

I was the first President killed while in office.

(LINCOLN)

? FACT CARD ?

A state is named after me. So is the capital city of the United States.

(WASHINGTON)

? FACT CARD ?

My picture is on the one dollar bill.

(WASHINGTON)

? FACT CARD ?

The country split into two parts after I became President.

(LINCOLN)

? FACT CARD ?

I crossed the Delaware River in a famous battle on Christmas in 1776.

(WASHINGTON)

? FACT CARD ?

I lived on a tobacco farm for much of my life.

(WASHINGTON)

? FACT CARD ?

My picture is on the five dollar bill.

(LINCOLN)

❓ FACT CARD ❓
I led the country during the Civil War.

(LINCOLN)

❓ FACT CARD ❓
I was once a Congressman from Illinois.

(LINCOLN)

❓ FACT CARD ❓
I was the first President to wear a beard in the White House.

(LINCOLN)

❓ FACT CARD ❓
I was famous for my tall black hat.

(LINCOLN)

❓ FACT CARD ❓
I wrote the Gettysburg Address. It praises the soldiers who died during the Civil War.

(LINCOLN)

❓ FACT CARD ❓
My nickname was "The Rail Splitter" because I was good at splitting wood for fences.

(LINCOLN)

❓ FACT CARD ❓
I signed a paper that freed the slaves in most of the South.

(LINCOLN)

❓ FACT CARD ❓
I worked as a lawyer in a town called Springfield.

(LINCOLN)

❓ FACT CARD ❓
The capital city of Nebraska is named after me.

(LINCOLN)

★ BONUS CARD ★
What country did the Americans fight in the Revolution?

(GREAT BRITAIN)

★ BONUS CARD ★
Where can you find the Lincoln Memorial?

(WASHINGTON, D.C.)

★ BONUS CARD ★
Name the day and month when Abrahan Lincoln was born.

(FEBRUARY 12)

★ BONUS CARD ★
Which two of these men did Washington know: Ben Franklin, John F. Kennedy, Thomas Jefferson?

(FRANKLIN AND JEFFERSON)

★ BONUS CARD ★
Who was George Washington's wife?

(MARTHA DANDRIDGE CUSTIS)

★ BONUS CARD ★
Name two jobs that Lincoln had before he became President.

(lawyer, clerk, Congressman, ferry-boat captain, rail splitter, farmhand)

★ BONUS CARD ★
Name the day and month when Washington was born.

(FEBRUARY 22)

★ BONUS CARD ★
What is Lincoln's most famous nickname?

(HONEST ABE)

★ BONUS CARD ★
Who was Abraham Lincoln's wife?

(MARY TODD)

Additional Resources

George Washington

George Washington by Ingri and Edgar d'Aulaire, Doubleday, 1936.

George Washington: Father of Our Country by David A. Adler, Holiday House, 1988.

George Washington's Breakfast by Jean Fritz, Putnam, 1984.

George Washington's Mother by Jean Fritz, Putnam, 1992.

Meet George Washington by Joan Heilbroner, Random House, 1989.

A Picture Book of George Washington by David A. Adler, Holiday House, 1989.

Washington's Birthday by Dennis B. Fradin, Enslow, 1990.

Abraham Lincoln

Abraham Lincoln: A Man for All the People by Myra Cohn Livingston, Holiday House, 1993.

Abraham Lincoln's Hat by Martha Brenner, Random House, 1994.

Honest Abe by Edith Kunhardt, Greenwillow, 1993.

Just a Few Words Mr. Lincoln: The Story of the Gettysburg Address by Jean Fritz, Putnam, 1993.

Lincoln's Birthday by Dennis B. Fradin, Enslow, 1990.

Meet Abraham Lincoln by Barbara Cary, Random House, 1989.

A Picture Book of Abraham Lincoln by David A. Adler, Holiday House, 1989.

Young Abraham Lincoln: The Frontier Days, 1809–1837 by Cheryl Harness, National Geographic Society, 1996.

Books for Teachers

Founding Father: Rediscovering George Washington by Richard Brookhiser, The Free Press, 1996.

George Washington: Man and Monument by Marcus Cunliffe, New American Library, 1982.

Lincoln by David Herbert Donald, Simon & Schuster, 1995.

Lincoln: An Illustrated Biography by B. Kunhardt, Knopf, 1992.